NATIVE AMERICAN CULTURES

A Study Unit to Promote Critical & Creative Thinking

Written by Rebecca Stark
Illustrated by Karen Neulinger

About the Cover Illustration:
On the cover is the artist's rendering of a Kwakiutl Echo mask. The spirit Echo was believed to have the ability to mimic the sounds made by any creature. The mask had several interchangeable mouth pieces, each used to represent a different figure. As he told Echo's tale, the wearer would replace Echo's mouth with the mouth of the creature Echo was imitating. Among the characters that could be portrayed by changing the mouth piece were Echo herself, Eagle, Raven, a bear, a fish, a human being, and an eagle.

The Kwakiutl lived in the Northwest Coast Culture Region in the area that is now British Columbia, Canada.

ISBN 0-910857-92-X

© 1992 Educational Impressions, Inc., Hawthorne, NJ

EDUCATIONAL IMPRESSIONS, INC.

Hawthorne, NJ 07507

Table of Contents

INTRODUCTION

This information-based, independent learning unit may be used for group, whole-class, or individual study. It is a comprehensive study unit on Native Americans. The focus is on the cultural aspects of these native peoples before the intrusion of the Europeans. One important exception to this emphasis is the Plains Indian culture, developed more fully after horses were introduced to the continent by the Spaniards.

The principal objective of this unit is to instill in youngsters an appreciation for the richness and diversity of the Native American heritage. When Columbus "discovered" America, there were about one million people—speaking about 300 different languages—living in North America. There are estimated to have been about 240 different tribal entities. The various cultures they developed reflect the differences in the ecological conditions of their environments.

Another important objective of this study unit is the development of crucial critical- and creative-thinking skills. The activities were specifically designed to encourage divergent thinking, flexibility of thought, fluent production of ideas, elaboration of details, and originality. They may be adjusted to suit your particular teaching style, time limitations, and/or the ability level of the children.

Rebecca Stark

The First Americans

Archaeologists—scientists who study the material remains of our past—had their first proof in 1926 that humans were in North America during the Ice Age. At a site near Folsom, New Mexico, a stone point was found between the ribs of an Ice Age bison. This find made it clear that the makers of the point (now called the Folsom People) and the bison lived at the same time. In the 1930s fluted spearpoints were found among the remains of mammoths and other now-extinct animals. The people who made them are now called Clovis People; they were named after the site of the discovery, Clovis, New Mexico. From these and other finds, archaeologists are certain that humans have been on the continent for at least 12,000 years. Some believe that they were there much longer than that. Part of the problem is that the carbon-14 testing—the usual method of dating—is not always accurate when testing bone.

In any case, the earliest Americans probably began to wander onto the American continent from Asia during the end of the last great Ice Age. At that time Asia and America were connected by an area of land that is now under water—an area we now call the Bering Strait. The small groups of nomadic hunters were probably following the woolly mammoth, giant sloth, and other prehistoric game upon which they depended for food, clothing, and shelter.

Today we call these first Americans Paleo-Indians. They continued to spread further and further south and east. Their descendents include the Mayas, Aztecs and Incas of Central and South America as well as the Shawnees, Iroquois, Cherokees, Sioux, Navajos, Pueblos and numerous other Indian peoples of North America.

Beyond a Reasonable Doubt

All living organisms contain a small amount of a radioactive element known as carbon-14. (Radioactive means it has the power to give off the type of energy called radiation.) While the organism is alive, it absorbs new carbon-14 at the same rate that it loses the carbon-14 it already absorbed. (It turns it into ordinary carbon.) Carbon-14 is useful in dating because once an organism has died, it no longer absorbs new carbon-14; however, it continues to lose the carbon-14 at a rate which is known. By measuring the amount of carbon-14, scientists can determine the approximate age of the object made with that material.

Carbon-14 has a half life of about 5,700 years. That means that 5,700 years after death, half of the carbon-14 atoms present in the animal or vegetable material will have disintegrated.

Assume that this represents the amount of radiation from a wooden beam that was just cut from a live tree.

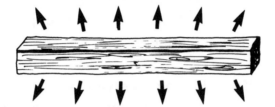

How old is this beam cut from a similar kind of tree? _____

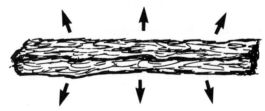

Unfortunately, testing is not always accurate. Think about and describe the possible problems which may arise.

_____

_____

_____

_____

_____

_____

A Case of Mistaken Identity

When Christopher Columbus sailed from Spain on August 3, 1492, he hoped to find a short route to the eastern lands known as the Indies. It was only natural for him to believe that those were the lands he and his men spotted on October 12 of that year. The natives they met, they called "Indians."

Of course, Columbus was wrong. The lands he had come upon were not the Indies; they were to him and the other Europeans who would follow a "New World"—a world that would become known as the Americas. The people living in the Americas—although they represented many different cultures— would continue to be called Indians by the white settlers and the Europeans.

By the time the Europeans arrived in North America, the Indians had already spread throughout the continent. The cultures they developed were based upon the natural resources of their particular environments. The diversity of those cultures were seen in their homes, clothing, food supplies, tools and weapons, arts and crafts, and religious practices.

Just as the Indians differed in their lifestyles, so did they vary in appearance. Although there were some characteristic traits shared by many tribes—black hair, tan or reddish-brown skin, and prominent cheekbones, for example—to generalize is a mistake. What's certain is that none of these people were red-skinned—that is, unless they were sunburned or painted red!

Also diverse were the languages of the North American Indians. The original number of languages spoken is believed to be about 300! These languages have been classified into related groups, or families. Among the many language families are Iroquoian, Athabascan, Algonquian, Souian, Yuman, Pomo, Caddoan, and Muskogean.

Anthropologists—scientists who study human beings and their cultures—estimate that there were at one time about 240 different tribes in North America. To make it easier to learn about these Native Americans, they grouped the tribes into larger culture areas. The main culture areas are the Northeast Woodlands, the Southeast, the Great Plains, the Southwest, California, the Great Basin, the Plateau, the Northwest Coast, and the Sub-Arctic.

Culture Areas of North America

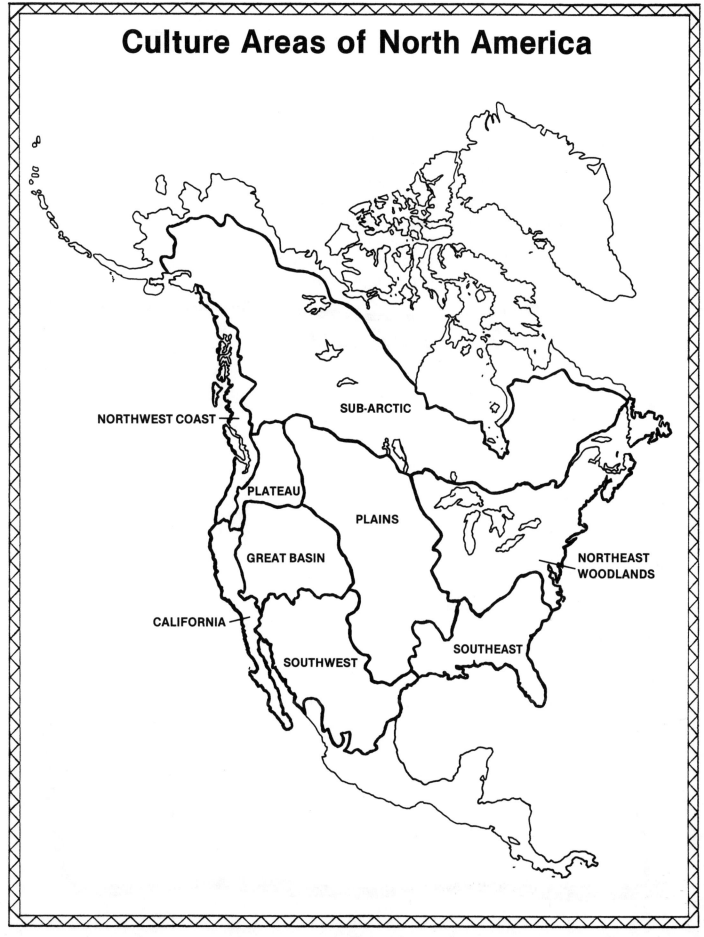

NORTHWEST COAST

SUB-ARCTIC

PLATEAU

PLAINS

GREAT BASIN

NORTHEAST
WOODLANDS

CALIFORNIA

SOUTHEAST

SOUTHWEST

Generosity: Repaid in Kind?

When Christopher Columbus sent back his first report, he wrote that the Indians he had met were "generous with what they have, to such a degree that no one would believe but he who had seen it. Of anything they have, if it be asked for, they never say no, but do rather invite the person to accept it, and show as much lovingness as though they would give their hearts...." In return, Columbus sent 500 of the Indians back to Spain as slaves and forced many others to work as slaves in the mines and plantations.

Write a letter to Christopher Columbus in which you describe your feelings regarding his treatment of the native peoples he met.

Dear Mr. Columbus,

History Re-Written

It is 1491. A group of Native Americans has crossed the Atlantic Ocean and landed somewhere in Europe. Upon seeing this New World (to them) for the first time, they claim to have discovered it.

Complete this political cartoon in a way that depicts the situation described above. (If you prefer, draw your cartoon on a separate sheet of paper.) Write at least three different punch lines to go with your cartoon.

_____

_____

_____

Choose the punch line you like the best. Write it in the balloon. (A balloon is the rounded or irregularly shaped outline in a cartoon. It contains the words a character in a cartoon is represented as saying.)

People of the Northeast Woodlands

The northeastern part of North America is covered with forests, lakes, rivers, and streams. They provided the Indians who lived in the region with animals to hunt, fish to catch, and wild plants to gather. They also provided them with the raw materials for their clothing, shelter, tools and weapons, transportation, and arts and crafts.

Although its importance varied, some agriculture was practiced throughout most of the region. The main crops were corn, beans, and squash. Among most of the tribes the women cultivated the fields, but the men usually helped to clear them.

A lot of tribes in the area were divided into social groups called clans. This was especially common in tribes where agriculture was very important. Members of a clan felt a sense of loyalty to one another and could be counted on to provide hospitality when visiting another community. Often, clans had animal names such as Deer, Wolf, Bear, or Hawk. This animal, called a totem, had a special relationship to the clan. Because members of a clan were thought to be related, members of the same clan could not marry one another.

Medicine societies played an important role in the Eastern Woodlands. The main function of these societies was to cure illness. Their memberships were made up of people who had themselves experienced such cures. Two of the best known Medicine Societies were the Midewiwin, or Great Medicine Society, of the Algonquins of the Great Lakes region and the False Face Society of the Iroquois.

People didn't always turn to a medicine society to seek a cure. Sometimes they went to a shaman. Shamans were believed to have the power to cure. They were made aware of this ability through a vision or a dream. Also, the people had an extensive knowledge of medicinal plants.

Wampum

Wampum beads were made from the white and purple quahog, or clam, shells found along the Atlantic shore. They were often woven into belts. These belts were used to record messages, treaties, and events. The designs served as memory devices. They helped the messenger remember all the details. Although wampum originated with the Algonquins, the Iroquois are best known for it.

Think about an important school, community, state, or national event that recently occurred. Design a wampum belt that would help you to remember the details of that event.

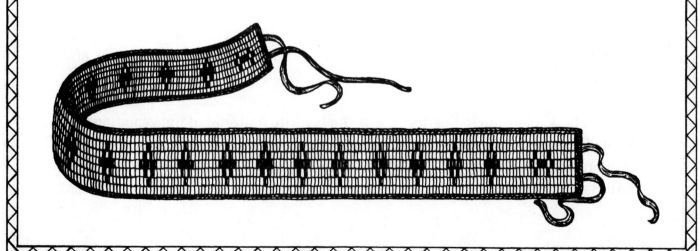

The Algonquian Hunters

Many of the tribes of the Eastern Woodlands were speakers of the Algonquian language. Among them were the Abnaki, Penobscot, Mohawk, Wampanoag, Mohegan, Mahican, Delaware, Powhattan, and Ojibwa (Chippewa). Although they did some farming, the Algonquins were mainly hunters. They lived mostly in bands of a few hundred people.

Because the Algonquian hunters had to move often to follow the animals, they needed homes that were easy to put up and take down. Many tribes built dome-shaped wigwams. Young trees, which are easy to bend, formed the framework. They were covered with bark and animal skins. Birch bark, which rolls easily, was used when available. A hole—which could be covered during a storm—was left in the center of the roof. Below the hole was a fire in a pit; the fire was used for cooking and for warmth. When it was time to move on, any large strips of birch bark were rolled up to be taken to the next location. The women did most of the work taking down and setting up the wigwams.

The Algonquian men, on the other hand, did the hunting and fishing. The main hunting season was fall through spring. They hunted deer, caribou, and other animals of the forests with their bows and stone-tipped arrows. Sometimes they used deadfalls to trap large animals. Small animals were often caught in snares. Fishing was a year-round activity. All sorts of fishing gear—including nets, spears, harpoons, and hooks—were used.

Depending on the location, other foods were also available. Water fowl were hunted on the lakes and rivers. Along the coast, the Indians gathered clams, oysters, mussels, and other sea life that came close to shore. In the Great Lakes region, wild rice was a main source of food. Also, mapling was important in many parts of the Northeast. The women and children collected the sap from the maple trees in birch bark troughs and boiled it down to make syrup and sugar.

Birch bark, plentiful in the north, was the favorite material of the Woodland Indians. Because it was easy to fold, the Algonquins used it to make most of their containers and cooking pots as well as their wigwams. It also provided the best material for canoes.

Just as the forests provided the Algonquins with food, shelter, and transportation, so did they provide them with the materials for their clothing. Most of the garments were made from animal skins, which the women stretched and tanned, or softened. Often, they decorated them with beautiful porcupine-quill embroidery.

The men wore leggings that were tight fitting and had short fringe so that they wouldn't get caught in the brush. They also wore a breechclout, which was a strip that hung over a belt in front and in back. A headdress called an artificial roach was popular for ceremonial occasions. It was made of moose, deer, or porcupine hair and was usually dyed red. Women wore a skirt and leggings. In colder weather they added a cape. Both men and women wore soft-soled moccasins. One reason they preferred soft soles was that they were easier to use with snowshoes, often necessary in the winter. Sometimes the people stuffed their moccasins with deer hair for extra warmth in the cold months.

The Algonquins believed in supernatural spirits that lived in every natural thing. These forces were called manitou. Manitou did not apply only to animate beings such as a deer or a bear. It also applied to inanimate things such as the sun, the moon, and the trees. Perhaps it is because they considered all of these natural things "beings" that they were so much "at one with nature."

Hidden Foods

The names of the following foods, commonly eaten by the Algonquins, are hiding in the sentences: beans, bear, caribou, clam, corn, deer, fish, maple, nut, and rabbit. Find the names and circle them.

EXAMPLE: meat

I'll be home at eight o'clock.

1. He made errors on the exam.

2. The voters gave Sam a pledge of loyalty.

3. Did the sailor cross the Pacific or not?

4. It was a tragic, lamentable situation.

5. The car I bought is a convertible.

6. Don't be a reckless driver.

7. Abe answered the telephone.

8. Jan utilized the health club's facilities often.

9. Jeff is here now.

10. The crab bit me on the finger.

Write five original sentences. In them hide the names of foods you like to eat.

_____

_____

_____

_____

_____

The Iroquois: People of the Longhouse

The word "Iroquois" is a French translation of an Algonquian word believed to mean "the enemy." Like many of the names we call the various tribes, "Iroquois" is not the name the people called themselves. They called themselves the Hodenosaunee, or "People of the House." Most of the Indian tribes called themselves names that meant "The People" or something similar.

The Iroquoian-speaking tribes of the Eastern Woodlands lived in permanent villages, often fenced in by a palisade. They dwelt in large elm-bark longhouses, each lodging several families. Down the center of the longhouse was a row of fires; each fire was shared by the families on either side of it.

When a child was born, it was considered a member of its mother's clan. Upon marriage, however, a man became a member of his wife's clan and moved into the longhouse with her family. We call this kind of society matrilineal.

Agriculture was very important to the Iroquois. The main crops were corn, beans, and squash. Because they could usually be seen growing side by side in the fields, these crops were often called the Three Sisters.

Because agriculture was so important, everyday life was very much regulated by the seasons. In the spring the men cleared the land and the women planted the seeds. In the summer the women tended the fields and in the fall they harvested the crops. A good harvest would provide enough for the long winter months.

The Iroquois held many celebrations in honor of the crops and the seasons. There were six main festivals: the Maple Festival, the Planting, the Strawberry, the Green Corn, the Harvest, and the New Year. Each involved several days of feasting, rituals, and long prayers of thanks.

After the harvest, families often went out on deer-hunting parties, which lasted until mid-winter. Hunting not only added to their food supply, but also provided skins, bone and horn. The skins were needed for their clothing and moccasins, and bone and horn provided the materials for their tools and utensils.

Although the women did most of the work in the fields, the men had other responsibilities. While the women tended the fields, the men hunted. They also built the houses and palisades, fished, and defended the villages against intruders. Sometimes they went on the warpath. In fact, the Iroquois warriors were among the fiercest and most feared of all.

Captives were sometimes killed and sometimes taken back to the village. Some of those who were brought back were tortured to death by members of the community. They tried their best to accept this treatment without crying out. Other captives were adopted into the tribe in order to replace members of their own tribe who had been killed. If adopted, they became loyal members of their new families.

For many years, the Iroquois battled one another as well as their Algonquian neighbors. Then, around the year 1570, five of the nations were united in the League of the Great Peace. The five nations were the Seneca, the Onondaga, the Cayuga, the Oneida, and the Mohawk. A pine tree was the League's symbol. (Later, when the Tuscarora moved to the region, they joined the confederacy. The league became known as the Six Nations instead of the Five Nations.) Under rule of the League, war could only be carried out against those tribes against whom the council had declared war. The council comprised fifty sachems, or peace chiefs. These sachems were men who had been chosen by the elder women of the nations. Each nation was allowed a set number of sachems.

The Iroquois believed that a great spiritual power, called orenda, was the essence of all natural things. Because contact with orenda was thought to be achieved through dreams, it was essential that dreams be obeyed. Orenda gave strength for everyday matters as well as sacred ones. It helped them live as they did—in harmony with nature!

Symbol of the Great League

A symbol is something that is used to represent something else—often an abstract idea. A pine tree was the symbol used to represent the Great League of the Iroquois. A flag is a symbol used to represent a nation. Try to think of many different kinds of symbols. List or draw those symbols and tell what each represents.

Formation of the League

The story of the formation of the League of the Great Peace is part fact and part myth. Before the League, there was much fighting amongst the Iroquois nations. The custom of revenge killings led to never-ending warfare. Some leaders among them, however, remembered the teachings of Teharonhiawagon, the Master of Life. Teharonhiawagon was believed to have been the first being on earth; he had commanded the people to love one another and to live in peace.

Among the leaders who proposed a council of peace was Hiawatha, who lived among the Onondagas. Opposed to him was a fierce and cruel Onondaga chief named Atotarho. Hiawatha left the land of the Onondagas and pleaded with the leaders of the Mowhawks, Oneidas, Senecas, and Cayugas to help restore peace among the Iroquois.

At this time a remarkable man named Deganawidah arrived from the land of the Hurons. (Deganawidah is probably a mythical figure.) He had had a vision. In this vision he saw a great spruce tree, reaching up to the sky. The tree had five roots and at its base was a snow-white carpet covering the countryside. The soil was composed of righteousness, justice, peace and the other principles of life as taught by Teharonhiawagon. Atop the tree was an eagle. Deganawidah interpreted his vision as a call from the Master of Life to unite humanity into a single family founded upon the Master's principles.

In some versions of this legend it is Deganawidah who converts Atotarho from an evil wizard and convinces him to join in peace. In many it is Hiawatha who combs the serpents of evil thoughts out of Atotarho's hair. (Although Atotarho was a real person, according to the legend he was twisted in mind and body and had serpents in his hair.) The name Hiawatha, in fact, means "he, the comber." In either case, Atotarho was reformed and was named firekeeper, the most important member of the new confederacy. Also, it was proclaimed that the land of the Onondagas would always be the place where the great council fire would burn.

A Mythical League

Research the facts behind the formation of the United Nations. Write a paragraph explaining these facts. Then create a myth to explain its formation. For example, perhaps one of the world leaders had a vision or a dream! You might want to mix fact with fiction. Be sure to stretch your imagination!

The real facts are:

_____

_____

_____

_____

_____

_____

HOW THE UNITED NATIONS CAME TO BE

People of the Southeast

The Southeast was made up of many different landscapes: mountains, plains, swamps, and seacoast. When the Europeans arrived, there were about 120,000 people living in the region! The people were farmers, hunters, fishermen, and gatherers. Most spoke the Muskhogean language, but there were speakers of the Natchez, Algonquian, Iroquoian, and Siouan languages as well.

Many Southeastern tribes had a well organized political system. Some towns had more than 1,000 people! Even in the Creek Confederacy, which covered 84,000 square miles and comprised fifty tribes, each individual town was fairly independent. In addition to the Creeks, tribes of the region included the Cherokees; the Chickasaws; the Natchez; the Choctaws; and the Seminoles, who were originally part of the Creek Confederacy.

The people often traveled by dugout. To make a dugout, a log was first hollowed out by fire. Stone axes, gouges, and chisels were used for the finishing work. So were shell scrapers. Tribes along the coast even went to sea in their dugouts.

Summers were long and hot. Little clothing was needed. Women wore skirts of skin or cloth. In cooler weather they sometimes added a tunic of mulberry bark. Men often wore a fringe of mulberry bark or a breechclout. Leggings were sometimes added to protect their legs from the underbrush.

Ceremonial occasions called for different clothing for the men. They often donned a robe covered with bird feathers. Special headdresses were usually worn. To show their authority, more important men also wore engraved shell disks, called gorgets, around their necks.

Warfare—in the form of raiding parties—was important here. It was part game, part ritual, and part status-seeking. The men often shaved their heads, leaving scalp locks as a challenge to take their scalps. Tattooing was also popular in many tribes. When a boy was first named, he was scratched. He was scratched again every time he proved himself as a warrior. Each exploit was recorded in the form of a design.

Each town claimed its surrounding territory as hunting grounds. Sometimes the men wore deer skins as they stalked the animals with their bows and cane arrows. Cane, which grows perfectly straight, was also used to make their blowguns, used to hunt small animals. Knives were fashioned by cutting a short length of cane on a slant.

Although the men helped clear the fields, the women did the farming. Maize, or corn, was the most important crop. The cornfields belonged to individual households, but generosity was encouraged. Some tribes had communal fields. Others required that each household donate a portion of the harvest to a public granary. The food was given to visitors, war parties, men leaving on public missions, and the needy.

The most important occasion was the Busk, or Green Corn Ceremony. It came with the ripening of the new crop. Until it was held, no new corn could be eaten. Included in the ceremony were singing, dancing, games, fasting, and feasting. Most tribes also included the drinking of a very strong beverage called the Black Drink. The Busk symbolized a fresh start. The sacred fire was re-kindled; new clothing, tools, and pottery were made; and old debts and grievances were forgiven!

The people believed that animals, plants, wind, rain, trees, and every other natural thing were inhabited by a spirit force. Animals, they believed, possessed souls. When disease came, it was because the hunters had failed to show respect to the souls of the animals. Plants, on the other hand, were the natural friends of humans. If disease did come, plants could be used to cure it. Death was thought to be caused by evil animal spirits, witches, or sorcerers. Most believed in an afterlife. To keep from being persuaded to join friends and relatives in death, elaborate funeral rites and taboos were practiced.

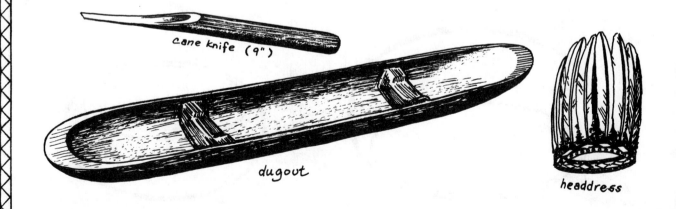

cane knife (9")

dugout

headdress

Chungke Stones

Chungke, an ancient game, was played all over North America. It was especially popular in the Southeast. Two players, each with a tapered eight-foot pole, ran down the field. One of them rolled on its edge a concave disk called a chungke stone. The chungke stone was about 5 inches in diameter and about an inch and a half thick. As they ran, they hurled their sticks and tried to land them as close as possible to the spot where the stone would stop rolling.

What can you make of these? Add details and use your imagination to make pictures of objects out of these chungke stones.

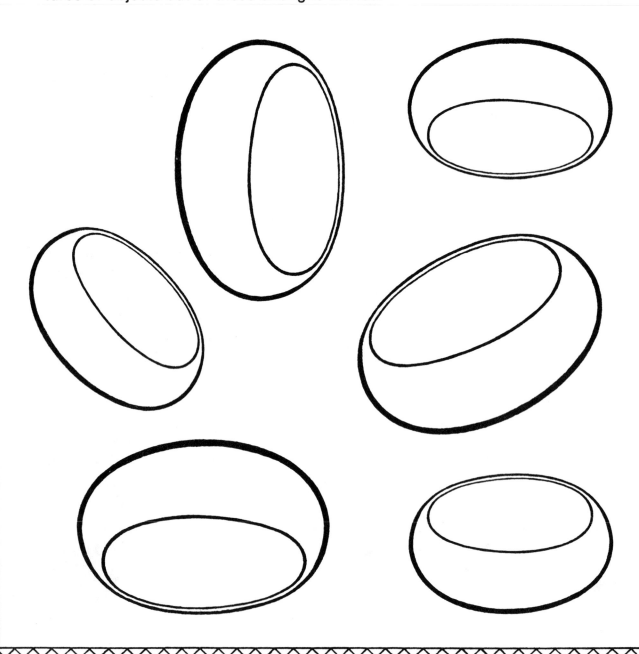

The Creek Confederacy

The largest group of Muskhogeans were the Creeks. The Creek Confederacy comprised about fifty tribes, or towns. Still, each town was fairly independent. Chieftainship was hereditary.

The central square, or plaza, of the town served as a meeting place. Built high on mounds within the square were the chief's houses. A public granary might also be found there.

The people's houses were outside the square. Most had at least a summer house and a winter house. The wealthy had four separate buildings: a small winter house, which was also used as a kitchen; an open summer house; and two storage bins.

Games and other forms of recreation were important. In one corner of the town was the Hot House, which was sealed tight except for a smoke hole. It was the men's winter recreation center. In another section was an open field where chungke was played. Popular in both the Northeast and the Southeast Woodlands was a form of racket-ball that became the forerunner of lacrosse. Played on a huge ball field, the game often involved hundreds of players.

In the Southeast, each player had two rackets per hand. The object was to get the ball between the opposing team's goal posts. Players caught, carried, and threw the ball, but could not touch it. It was a very rough game in which the rackets were often used as clubs! Among the Creeks, there were two teams of about sixty men each. The Red Creeks, who represented war, played against the White Creeks, who represented peace. The games were so important that arguments over territory were often settled by their outcome!

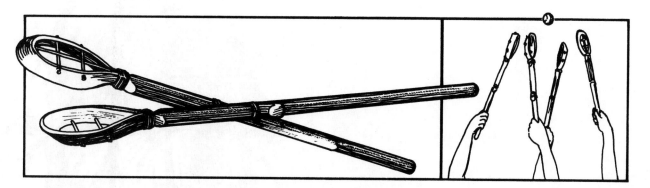

War Games: A New Meaning

What if a current dispute between two nations or groups could be settled by the outcome of a game! Write a proposal to the two parties involved in the dispute. Review the basic problems of the dispute. Explain the game to be played, the rules of the game, the stakes, and so on. Try to convince each side of the benefits of settling in this manner.

The Seminoles

The Seminoles were originally part of the Creek Confederacy. In the late 1700's they migrated into Florida from Georgia. There they mingled with slaves and other refugees. Florida was under Spanish rule. According to Spanish law, any foreign slave who entered the territory became free upon entrance.

The Seminoles were basically hunters and fishers. It was hot most of the year. Their homes, called chickees, were a lot like the summer houses of the northern Creek tribes. They had open sides and thatched roofs and were built high on stilts as protection against the wet ground and the snakes.

Seminole clothing showed a great deal of European influence. It was decorated with bright colored strips to resemble the brocaded clothing of the Spaniards. The women wore many strings of beads. As young girls they received one string per year. They continued to receive them until they were middle aged. Then they gave back a string each year.

In an effort to keep their lands, the Seminoles fought a series of wars against the United States government. The First Seminole War (1817-18) was fought over attempts by the United States to recapture runaway black slaves who were living among the Seminoles. As a result of that war, Spain ceded Florida to the United States. The Second Seminole War (1835-42) was an attempt by the Seminoles to keep from being forced to move to Indian Territory—the present state of Oklahoma. Although the war was long and costly to the United States, most of the Seminoles finally surrendered and emigrated to Indian Territory.

It was during the Second Seminole War that Indian patriot Osceola played an important role. A group of Seminoles who refused to be moved had withdrawn into the malaria-ridden swamps of the Everglades. Led by Osceola, a Creek who had moved from Georgia to Florida, these Indians fought bravely against the larger American army.

The fighting had gone on for two years when Osceola, accompanied by about 200 warriors, went to St. Augustine under a flag of truce. The army commander, General Jesup, had agreed to meet with him. Instead, the general ordered that the Indians be seized and imprisoned. Osceola was removed to Fort Moultrie at Charleston, South Carolina. He died there on January 30, 1838. He was 34.

Ode to a Patriot Warrior

An ode is a poem of praise that expresses the poet's feelings about a person, object or quality. The length of the lines, number of lines, number of stanzas, and the rhyming patterns are up to the individual poet.

Even his former enemies spoke highly of the brave Osceola. Create an ode in his praise.

ODE TO OSCEOLA

The Cherokee

The Cherokee nation, one of the largest in the Southeast was not Muskhogean, but Iroquoian. Like most Southeastern tribes, the Cherokee were farmers, hunters, fishers, and gatherers. In the center of their town was the town square. High on a mound was a 7-sided council house, where the town chief met with his counselors.

The people lived in houses scattered around the square. Like the Creeks, many had more than one house. Because it was cold in the mountainous regions where the Cherokee lived, families often gathered around the fire in the center of the house.

Each family was given a field to work according to its needs. A large family got a large field; a small family got a smaller one. All the men worked together to clear the fields. If someone was too old or too sick, his work was done for him.

In 1809 a Cherokee by the name of Sequoya began working on an alphabet, or syllabary, for the Cherokee language. When he completed his work in 1821, there were 86 characters. At first the people accused him of witchcraft, but he soon convinced them of its usefulness. Before long, thousands of Cherokee could read and write! Books and newspapers were published in the Cherokee language. Sequoya had made the Cherokee a literate nation!

A Literacy Award

Design an award that might be presented in honor of Sequoya for his contribution to the Cherokee nation. Be sure to include an inscription that tells why his contribution was such an important one.

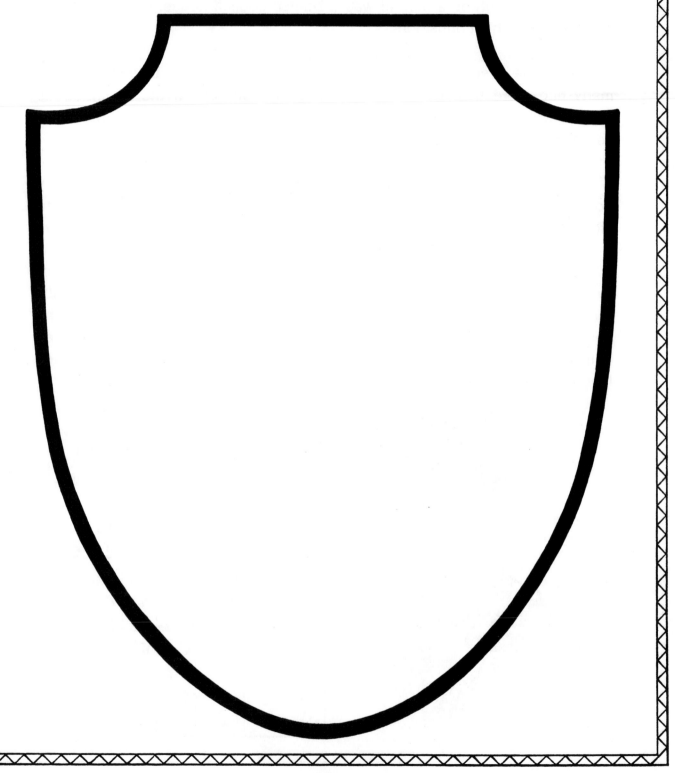

The Trail of Tears

In 1830 the United States government passed the Indian Removal Act. It gave the President the right to exchange western land for Indian land within the states. The new Indian Territory—now the state of Oklahoma—was considered unfit for white settlers.

Some of the Northern tribes went peacefully to these new lands. In the Southeast, however, most refused. The Cherokee, Chickasaw, Choctaw, Creek, and Seminole tribes—by then known as the Five Civilized Tribes—did not want to give up their homes and their farms!

Although force was not provided for in the original bill, it was eventually used. About 100,000 people were forced to abandon their lands. They were marched by United States troops across the country to Indian Territory. Almost a fourth of them died along the way. The Cherokee call their terrible trek of 1838-39 the "Trail of Tears."

A Letter to the President

The Cherokee resisted their removal from their home lands to Indian Territory as long as they could. They made appeal after appeal in the white man's court and finally won their case in the U. S. Supreme Court. Chief Justice Marshall denounced the wrongs that had been done to the Cherokee by the state of Georgia and declared that the acts forcing the Indians out were unconstitutional. The Cherokee were ecstatic—but their celebrations were short-lived. President Jackson refused to act upon the decision of the Supreme Court!

Write a letter to President Jackson. Tell why you agree or disagree with his decison not to carry out Chief Justice Marshall's ruling.

Dear Mr. President,

The Natchez

The Natchez, who lived in the Southeast, descended from the ancient Temple Builders and built their temples on great mounds. They were divided into four classes: Suns; Nobles; Honored People; and Commoners (the French translated the Indian term to mean Stinkards). Their ruler, the Great Sun, was believed to be descended from the sun itself. He was so sacred that he had to be carried around on a litter so that his feet would not touch the ground.

Children of the three higher classes had the rank of their mother. Children of commoner mothers ranked one class below that of their father. Suns could only marry commoners. Even the Great Sun himself had a sun mother and a commoner father!

That's My Boy

The Great Sun allowed only his wife to eat at his table. He pushed his leftovers to his brothers and other relatives with his feet. Anyone who wished to speak to him had to keep at least four paces away. He was carried in a litter so that his feet wouldn't touch the ground. If it were necessary for him to walk, mats were placed under his feet. He had absolute authority.

Write an entry in a diary as if written by the commoner father of the Great Sun.

Dear Diary,

People of the Plains

Before the coming of the Europeans, hundreds of tribes, speaking many different languages, inhabited the wide open spaces of the Great Plains. The early tribes settled in the eastern Plains, where the soil was rich and rainfall was dependable. There they farmed the fertile land, made pottery, and established large stockaded villages. These villages were often set on a cliff high above a river so that the villagers could see who approached.

Northern tribes like the Mandan and the Pawnee built large sturdy earth lodges. The lodges had log frameworks and were covered with grass, earth, and sod to protect them from the severe winters. Many families—and their animals—shared a lodge. A central fire provided heat and light. Above it was a smoke hole; when it rained, the hole was covered with one of their round skin boats. In nice weather, many people gathered on the roofs to enjoy the sun.

At that time huge herds of buffalo roamed the Western Plains. When the herds came close to the villages, the men left to follow them. The hunt was filled with danger. Often some ran the herd over cliffs or into corrals while others waited with their bows and arrows.

Their traveling homes were tepees, which could easily be set up and taken down. A tepee was built by setting up a framework of poles and covering it with tanned cow-buffalo skins which had been sewn together. Tepees stayed cool in summer and warm in winter.

The Indians transported their tepees and other belongings by means of a travois. It was made by fastening two tepee poles to a dog and placing the load across them. The tepee couldn't be too large or the dog wouldn't be able to drag the poles.

When horses, which had been brought to the New World by the Spaniards, arrived on the Plains, life changed. The horse travois made it possible to transport larger tepees. Now whole families could travel together. The men painted the outside of the tepees with pictures representing their totems and their exploits. The women painted the inside with beautiful geometric designs.

Tribes such as the Sioux, Blackfoot, Cheyenne and—above all—the Comanche became expert riders. Now they could hunt the buffalo on horseback. The hunt became the most important activity on the Plains. The buffalo provided much more than food. The skins were made into clothing, moccasins, tepees, blankets, shields, and containers. Bones, teeth, and horns provided the materials for many tools and weapons. Sinew became cord. Even the stomach was utilized; it was used as a container for cooking!

With these and other needs met by the buffalo, there was more time for leisure—and for war! Some of the raids were carried out to steal horses. Many were fought for adventure and glory. It was more important for a warrior to take risks and to show his bravery than to kill enemies. Making a coup, or touching the enemy, was the most important of all. Some carried special poles adorned with feathers with which to do this. They were called coup sticks. After a battle, the warriors would tell and retell accounts of their brave deeds. Boasting was acceptable as long as the details were accurate.

The bravest warriors wore bonnets of eagle feathers. Each feather represented a coup. Warriors also wore special war shirts and carried special shields. The shirts were decorated with the warrior's outstanding deeds. The shields were made from the shrunken thick neck skin of the buffalo. Their designs were believed to have magical powers that would protect their owners in battle. These designs usually came to the warrior in a vision or dream.

Visions were very important on the Plains. A young man sat alone for days, fasting and praying for a vision. Often he dreamed of an animal that would be his protector. A vision might also tell him what objects to put together in his sacred medicine bundle.

The Plains Indians had many ceremonies. The most important was probably the one we call the Sun Dance. Usually, it was held to fulfill a vow someone had made to the spirits during a time of distress. After fasting and undergoing purification in the sweat lodge, the dancers gathered in a circular shed made with poles with leafy branches. They did a slow stomp dance around a center tree that had been cut down to represent a slain enemy. For four days the dancers went without food or water. Some tribes also included a form of self-torture.

The culture of the Plains was a rich one. At night people gathered around and listened to the storyteller relate tales about great hunters and great warriors. They listened to stories of supernatural animals and birds and other spirits—stories that would carry on the great traditions of life on the Plains.

A Practical Wardrobe

The men hunted the buffalo, but the Plains women worked the hides. They cleaned, stretched, and softened them. Then they used them to make not only their tepees, but also their beautiful, yet practical clothing.

During most of the year, men wore a breechclout, leggings with long fringe, and moccasins. Unlike Indians in other areas of North America, the Plains Indians had moccasins with hard, rawhide soles that matched their right and left feet. Women wore deerskin dresses with knee-high leggings and moccasins. In the winter both men and women used robes and blankets with the fur left on for extra warmth. The fur was worn on the inside; the outside was often painted. Men painted theirs with symbols representing their brave deeds. Many women painted theirs with a sunburst design.

Women often decorated their clothing and other belongings with dyed porcupine quills. When the Indians began to trade with the Europeans for glass beads, they became skilled at beadwork as well. Before long beadwork was more popular than quillwork. Elks' teeth were especially prized as decoration for a woman's dress. Because only a few teeth from a single elk could be used, a dress with a lot of teeth meant that the woman's husband was a fine hunter.

My Bravest Deed

Decorate this winter robe with a picture representing your bravest deed.

What Did You Say?

Sign language was very important on the Plains. The quick movements of the hand were readily recognized by all the tribes. Analyze the reasons that sign language was important.

A Pretty, Practical, Painted Parfleche

The Indians of the Plains carried many of their belongings in a practical buffalo-hide container known as a parfleche. It could easily be carried on horseback and was very practical for people who moved around so much.

Among the items carried in a parfleche was often pemmican. Pemmican was a mixture of dried buffalo meat, fat and wild berries all pounded together. It could be stored almost indefinitely.

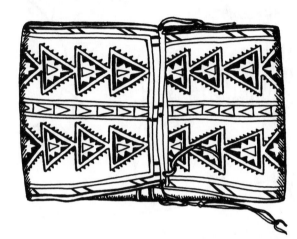

Please put the pounded pemmican in the pretty, practical, painted parfleche.

The above sentence is an example of alliteration. Alliteration is the repetition of a sound at the beginning of two or more neighboring words. It is also an example of a tongue twister. A tongue twister is a sentence that is difficult to say clearly because of the succession of similar consonant sounds. (Try to say the sentence quickly three times in a row!) Many tribes, such as the Crow, enjoyed saying tongue twisters as quickly as possible while trying to avoid error.

Write five original tongue twisters. If possible, have at least three of them tell an important or interesting fact about an Indian tribe.

_____

_____

_____

_____

_____

Two Winters Ago...

The Plains Indians recorded the history of their tribe by painting on a buffalo hide a figure representing the most important event of the year. Each year a figure was added in a spiral. These hides are called winter counts because the people kept track of time by the number of winters that passed.

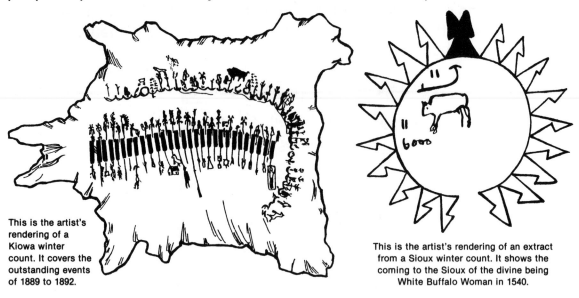

This is the artist's rendering of a Kiowa winter count. It covers the outstanding events of 1889 to 1892.

This is the artist's rendering of an extract from a Sioux winter count. It shows the coming to the Sioux of the divine being White Buffalo Woman in 1540.

The Story of My Life

Think ahead to the future. You are eighty years old. You have had a rich and rewarding life. Although you have had your ups and downs, many of your childhood dreams have been fulfilled. Make a winter count representing the most important events of your long, basically happy life. (You do not have to include every year!)

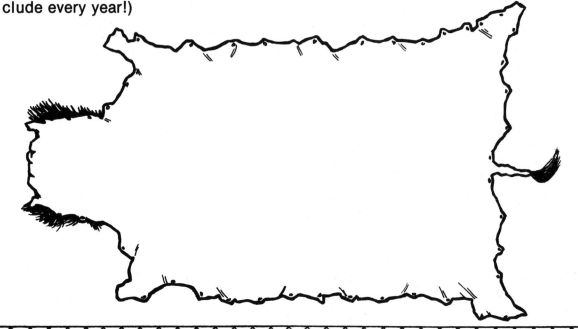

People of the Southwest

The southwestern part of North America is a land of steep canyons and dry deserts—a land of little rainfall. It wouldn't seem that this environment would support a large population. Yet, Indians have lived in this region for thousands of years, and many of their cultures have been based upon farming. What's more, their farms flourished. Those who lived near rivers developed irrigation works to bring water to their fields. Others became skilled at dry farming.

There were four main groupings of Southwestern Indians: the Yuma; the Pima and the Papago; the Pueblo; and the Apache and the Navajo. The Yuma farmed the fields made rich by the flooding and silting of the Colorado River every spring. The Pima and the Papago took advantage of river flooding too; however, they also built canals to irrigate even larger areas of land. The Pueblo men planted their fields over underground streams; they also learned other practices to make the most of the little moisture that was available on the high, semi-arid Colorado Plateau. The Navajo, a branch of the Athabascan-speaking Apache, were latecomers to the region. At first they were hunters and gatherers who wandered from place to place. After a while, however, they adapted many of the Pueblos' ways; they became farmers and herders and eventually settled down.

The lifestyles, social structures, and belief systems of the tribes in the Southwest varied. Each developed a way of life suited to the problems of survival in its own particular geographic surroundings. Each adapted to its environment as best it could.

Picture Writing

Early Indians carved pictures in the smooth walls of the cliffs and caves. On the rock below draw symbols that tell a story. Have your classmates guess what the pictures mean.

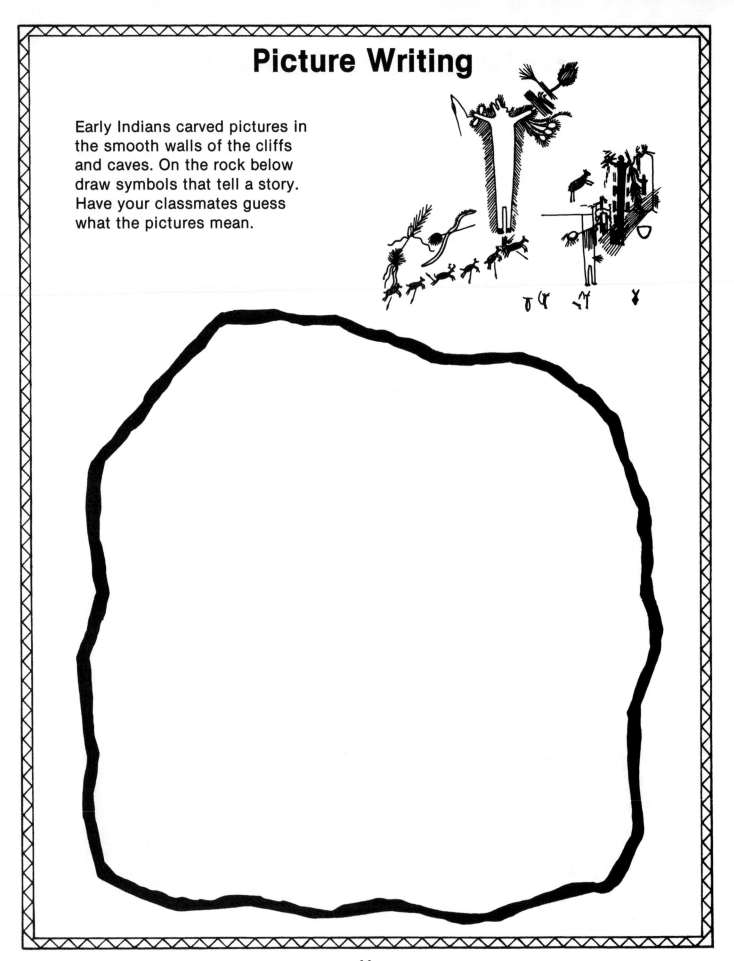

The Pueblo Townspeople

The various Pueblo tribes spoke several different languages, but they shared many of the same cultural traits. There are three Pueblo sub-groups: the western Pueblos, including the Hopi and the Zuni; the central Pueblos, including the Santa Ana and the Zia; and the eastern Pueblos, including the San Ildefonso and the Taos.

Although it would not seem that the Southwest—with its steep canyons and hot deserts—would be suited for farming, many of the tribes had farms that flourished. The peaceful Pueblo farmers descended from the ancient Indians known as the Anasazi. Unlike most other Indian farming cultures, here the men and boys planted and harvested the fields of corn, beans, squash, and cotton.

The men also wove the cotton into cloth, sometimes mixing it with rabbit fur, feathers, or dog hair. The cloth was then used to make kilts and sashes for the men and cotton dresses, dyed blue with sunflower seeds, for the women.

Pueblo women became excellent potters. The shapes of their pottery were not only beautiful, but also practical. The women created water-storage jars, bowls, cooking pots, and other useful containers. They decorated them using brushes made from yucca leaves and colors made from colored earths.

The Pueblos lived in apartment-like homes, also called pueblos. ("Pueblo" is the Spanish word for "town.") They were built of stone and adobe, a special kind of clay. The women did much of the building and plastering. The houses were several stories high, often in a step design. Many were built high on cliffs as protection from raiders. The people climbed up ladders and went in through a hole in the roof. When enemies approached, the ladders were pulled up.

Each clan had a certain section of the pueblo. The clan gave out rooms to the families according to their needs. In one room was a bin to grind the corn, their staple food. The women ground the corn with a large, flat stone called a metate. They knew many different ways to cook the corn. One especially delicious way was to make paper-thin pancakes called piki. To make it a woman dipped her hand into the batter and spread it quickly over a very hot stone. She had to be quick and careful or she would get burned!

Sometimes the men added to the food supply by hunting with bows and arrows. Pronghorn antelope were the most important game, but small game was also taken. Rabbit hunts, using curved throwing sticks, were commonly held. Even young boys could participate.

An important part of every pueblo was the underground chamber called a kiva. It served as a meeting place for the men. More importantly, it was the place where many secret rituals were held.

The Pueblos had many ceremonies. They believed in kachina spirits who lived among the people for half the year—from July until January. The kachinas were messengers between the gods and the people. Dancers wore kachina masks of deer or buffalo hide and performed carefully rehearsed rituals.

These ceremonies—like all Pueblo rituals—reflected the importance of every person, animal, plant and superbeing in the scheme of things. The Pueblos believed that without the active participation of all these beings, the life-giving sun would not return from his winter home; the rain would not come; and the crops would not grow. In short, life would cease to exist.

The Snake Ceremony

An important ceremony for the Hopi was the Snake Ceremony. Find out more about the Snake Ceremony. Tell about this ritual from the point of view of one of the snakes.

The Navajos

Compared to the Pueblos, the Navajos were latecomers to the Southwest. At first they roamed the area, hunting and gathering. They learned a lot from the Pueblos and adapted what they learned. The Navajos became farmers and later herders. Their homes, called hogans, were originally simple earth lodges with a framework like a tepee. Later on they built them as six- or eight-sided log buildings with dirt roofs.

The Navajos learned to weave from the Pueblos. Unlike their teachers, however, the women did the weaving. They wove beautiful blankets, passing down their designs from mother to daughter. The women also abandoned their buckskin dresses and adopted the handwoven dresses of the Pueblos; however, they made them in two pieces rather than one and added stripes.

Even sand painting, which became so important to the Navajos, was adapted from the Pueblos. The Navajos believed that everything in nature must be in harmony. Illness was the surest sign of disharmony; therefore, they held elaborate healing ceremonies. A sand painter dropped dry pigments, charcoal, and powdered stone onto a bed of clean sand. The sick person sat in the middle of the painting. Pinches of it were placed on the patient's body. The gods symbolized in the painting were believed to enter the sick body and cure it. The painting had to be destroyed by sunset of the day it was begun.

The Navajos borrowed from their neighbors many cultural traits: farming, herding, weaving, and sand painting. They changed them, adapted them to fit their needs, and made them their own!

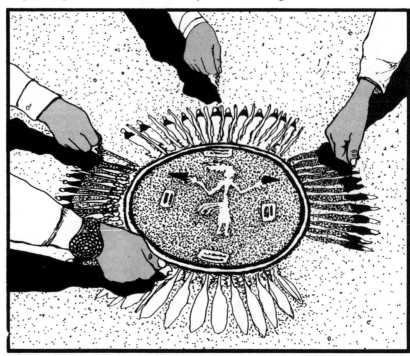

The String Game

The string game, often called cat's cradle, was very popular among the Navajos. They often spent hours making intricate patterns. They used not only their hands, but also their teeth, sticks, stones, and anything else they needed to hold the string in place.

Like many other Indian games, weaving string patterns had magical and ritual significance. The Navajos believed that the string game, with its intricate, web-like patterns, was taught to their ancestors. Other tribes had other explanations. Zuni mythology associated it with the netted shield of their war gods; they believed the game was taught to the war gods by their grandmother, the Spider.

Invent an original mythical explanation of the origin of the string game.

The Apache Raiders

The Apaches traveled together in small bands. Some of the tribes looked and dressed much like the tribes of the Great Plains. They were mainly hunters and gatherers, but a few did some farming. Most of the men were skilled horsemen and fierce warriors.

The training of young warriors was harsh and intense. Often they were made to run several miles in the heat with a mouthful of water. They could not swallow the water. Other times they practiced dodging arrows.

Many Apaches lived in dwellings called wickiups. They were made of branches and grass laid over a framework of poles. In times of peace, the wickiups were sturdy and well made. In times of war they were usually crude shelters quickly thrown together. They could break camp in a matter of minutes.

The Apaches believed that in every natural thing—every plant, tree, mountain, and rock—there existed a power. Each power source could cause either good or evil. Their ceremonies, therefore, were intended to convince these powers to cure disease and to bring success in hunting and in warfare. One of their most important rituals was the Mountain Spirit Ceremony. The performers impersonated the Mountain Spirits believed to live in the sacred mountains. Part of the ceremony to ward off evil was the Apache Fire Dance.

The culture of the Apaches was unlike that of the other Southwestern tribes. Like them, however, they used the land and its resources in the best way they knew how. Like them, they tried to live in harmony with nature.

Find Those Words

The Jicarilla, the Chiricahua, the Kiowa, and the Mescalero are four important Apache tribes.

There are at least 90 words hidden in the word "Mescalero." See how many you can find! You may use a letter more than once only if it is in the word "Mescalero" more than once. You may not use the "s" to form the plural of a word if the singular form has been used. Good luck!

M-E-S-C-A-L-E-R-O

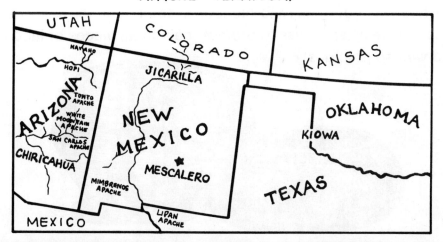

APACHE TERRITORY

People of California

Although in land size California represented the smallest culture area, it was the most highly populated. When the Europeans arrived, there were probably more than 275,000 people living in the region. They spoke more languages and formed more separate groups than in any other part of North America.

Because of the warm climate, their clothing was simple. The men wore a simple buckskin breechclout, if anything. The women wore a small double apron of bark fiber. Sometimes they wore a brimless hat, which was really an upside-down basket. In the hills, where the weather was cooler, the people often added grass or buckskin sandals and maybe even a fur cloak.

Their homes were also simple. Most were small, domed houses with a framework of bent poles. The poles were covered with grass and rushes. Their sweat lodges, however, were covered with earth and were larger and sturdier. These lodges served as a clubhouses for the men.

The California Indians hunted and fished, but they were basically gatherers. Acorns were their most important food source. Although acorns are bitter, the people knew how to get rid of that bitterness.

They gathered the acorns and other foods in their beautifully crafted baskets. Although the men did some basketry, the women did the finest work. They made containers of all sizes: from just a few inches to many feet in diameter.

In spring and summer the people were widely scattered. In winter, however, they often came together in villages. Most villages had peace chiefs and war chiefs. Warfare was not usually to plunder or to gain honor as it was in other culture areas. More often, it was to protect their small pieces of land in an area where land was so precious!

Coyote Makes Man

Folktales were an integral part of the social and cultural life of the native peoples of North America. The tales were enhanced by the imaginative skills of the narrators. The Californians had many elaborate creation tales. The following is a Yokuts legend. First figure out the code. Then re-write the story of how Man was created by Coyote.

XLBLGV NZPVH NZM

XLBLGV DRHSVW GL XIVZGV NZM. SV XZOOVW ZOO GSV ZMRNZOH LU VZIGS GLTVGSVI GL ZHP GSVRI ZWERXV. VZXS GLOW GSV UVZGFIV RG GSLFTSG NZM HSLFOW YV TREVM. ORLM HFTTVHGVW Z ELRXV GSZG XZM ILZI, HSZIK GVVGS ZMW XOZDH. TIRAAOB YVZI HFTTVHGVW TIVZG HGIVMTGS. WVVI HFTTVHGVW YVZFGRUFO OLMT SLIMH, DSROV NLFMGZRM TLZG HFTTVHGVW GSZG GSV SLIMH YV ILOOVW. LDO HFTTVHGVW DRMTH, ZMW NLFHV HFTTVHGVW HSZIK VBVH. XLBLGV ORHGVMVW GL GSV ZWERXV. "ZOO LU BLF ZIV EVIB ULLORHS," SV HZRW. "BLF ZOO DZMG GL NZPV NZM ORPV BLFIHVOEVH. NZM HSLFOW YV GSVHV GSRMTH," SV ZTIVVW, "YFG SV HSLFOW ZOHL YV ZH DRHV ZH R ZN."

GSV ZMRNZOH VZXS DLIPVW GL NZPV NZM LFG LU XOZB. VZXS GIRVW GL NZPV NZM OLLP ORPV SRNHVOU. YFG YVULIV GSVB XLFOW URMRHS, GSVB ZOO UVOO ZHOVVK. XLBLGV GSIVD DZGVI LM GSV XOZB URTFIV ZMW GSVB ZOO NVOGVW ZDZB. YB GSV GRNV GSV ZMRNZOH ZDZPVMVW, XLBLGV SZW XIVZGVW NZM. SV SZW TREVM GL NZM GSV YVHG KZIG LU VZXS LU GSV ZMRNZOH.

53

People of the Great Basin

West of the Rocky Mountains, where Nevada and Utah are today, in the area called the Great Basin, life was hard. It was dry most of the year. Then, when it finally rained, it came down in torrents. Summers were extremely hot and winters extremely cold. It was in this environment that the Paiutes, Shoshones, and Washos did their best to adjust and survive. They built crude huts, called wickiups, for shelter. Food was scarce. The people wandered in small family groups and searched for nuts, seeds, insects, and roots to eat. Occasionally, the bands gathered for communal locust or rabbit hunts. Survival was difficult.

By 1800 several of the tribes in the northern and eastern parts of the Great Basin got horses. For those tribes, life got easier. Their lifestyles took on many characteristics of the Plains culture area.

Sacajawea

Sacajawea, a young Shoshone, was living among the Mandans in the northern Plains when Meriwether Lewis and William Clark first met her. They had hired her husband, Toussaint Charbonneau, to be their interpreter. He was to help them in their dealings with the Indians they would meet as they continued to explore the newly purchased Louisiana Territory.

Sacajawea was very helpful to Lewis and Clark in many ways. She acted as their guide. She helped them find wild roots to balance their diets. She helped them obtain horses from the Shoshone when they arrived at the land of her people. She and her two-year-old child helped them convince the Indians they met that their mission was a peaceful one.

When Captain Lewis first agreed to allow Sacajawea and her son join their party, he was very reluctant. He had no idea how important she would be to their expedition. No one could have guessed that she would some day be considered a hero throughout the land!

A Difficult Decision

Sacajawea had been kidnapped from the Shoshone as a child and later sold to the Mandans. When the expedition party arrived at Shoshone country, Sacajawea learned that the chief of the band was her brother Cameahwait. She hadn't seen him in years. Cameahwait sold five horses to the party and agreed to sell them more. These horses were vital to the success of the expedition. Sacajawea found out that her brother planned to back out of the deal; his people were starving and he had learned that there was a buffalo herd nearby. He needed the horses for the hunt. Sacajawea did not want to betray her brother. On the other hand, she knew that the expedition could not continue without the horses. She told her husband, who told Captain Lewis. With Sacajawea as interpreter, Lewis convinced Cameahwait to sell the horses as promised.

A soliloquy is a speech that gives the impression that one is talking to oneself. Write a soliloquy as if being said by Sacajawea as she is deciding whether or not to reveal her brother's plan to back out of his promise.

People of the Plateau

The Plateau was bordered by the Rocky Mountains, the Cascades, and the Pacific Coast. Conditions in this region were similar to those of the Great Basin area to the south; however, they were not as harsh.

In the Plateau were two great rivers, the Columbia and the Fraser. They provided the people with salmon, their primary source of food. Other fish and wild plants supplemented their diets. Sometimes deer, elk, game birds, and mountain sheep were also available. Besides providing more food, the availability of these animals also made it possible for the people to have more clothing here than in the Basin.

Some of the tribes, like the Nez Percé, Cayuse, Wallawalla, and Flathead, eventually obtained horses. Their lifestyles then changed. More and more they took on the characteristics of the Plains Indians; however most remained more peaceful than the Plains tribes. They hunted the buffalo that roamed onto the Plateau and occasionally rode onto the Plains for a hunt.

The Plateau Indians believed in a great spirit as well as spirits of the atmosphere, such as wind and thunder, and animal spirits that served as guardians. Many rituals involved the guardian-spirit quest. All boys and some girls participated. They believed that in adult life their guardian spirit would reappear. These guardian spirits were very specialized. For example, some turned the people they guarded into warriors; some turned them into hunters; and still others turned them into medicine men. A Spirit Dance was held in the winter. Participants of the ceremony personified their guardian spirits. Many believed that successful performances would bring about warm weather, abundant food supplies, and a successful hunting season!

Chief Joseph of the Nez Percés

The Nez Percés had lived in peace with the white people since their first contact with them in 1805, when the Lewis and Clark Expedition traveled through their lands. Even when neighboring tribes were warring with the whites, the Nez Percés avoided getting involved.

In 1855 several Nez Percés chiefs signed a treaty with the United States government that designated a large area as a reservation for the tribe. In 1860, when white trespassers found gold on the reservation, thousands of white settlers and miners moved in and pushed the Indians out. The government tried to force the Nez Percés to accept a new, much smaller reservation. Although some agreed, most of the chiefs refused to sign the revised treaty.

In 1871 Chief Joseph, upon the death of his father, took over leadership of his band. In 1877 the Indian Bureau gave those who had not agreed to the revised treaty an ultimatum—either move to the new reservation or be placed there by force! Chief Joseph hated to give up their land, but he believed that it was better to "live at peace than to begin a war and lie dead." He agreed to lead the removal of his people to the new reservation.

Finally, however, a series of raids on both sides led to war. Once forced to fight, Chief Joseph proved to be as great a military leader as he had been a statesman. Time after time he outmanuevered U.S. troops. In the end, however, he and his people surrendered. The Nez Percés were forced to leave their mountain homes and to relocate in the barren flatlands of Indian Territory.

Not Theirs to Sell

The U.S. commissioners insisted that the Nez Percés had sold their land to the U.S. government. Chief Joseph gave this eloquent reply:

> If we ever owned the land we own it still, for we never sold it. In the treaty councils the commissioners have claimed that our country has been sold to the government. Suppose a white man should come to me and say, "Joseph, I like your horses, and I want to buy them." I say to him, "No, my horses suit me; I will not sell them." Then he goes to my neighbor, and he says to him, "Joseph has some good horses. I want to buy them, but he refuses to sell." My neighbor answers, "Pay me the money and I will sell you Joseph's horses." The white man returns to me and says, "Joseph, I have bought your horses and you must let me have them." If we sold our lands to the government, this is the way they were bought.*

A STORY STARTER—Write an original story based upon the following scenario: You and your family are enjoying a relaxing day at home. Unexpectedly, the doorbell rings. At your front door is a family of four. A moving van with all their belongings is parked in your driveway. When you ask what's going on, they insist that they are moving into your home. They explain that your neighbor sold them your house!

Write your story on another sheet of paper.

*See Josephy, Alvin M. (New York: Viking Press, 1961), pp. 322-323.

People of the Northwest Coast

Along the Northwest Coast only a narrow strip of land runs between the Pacific Ocean and the heavily wooded mountains. It was on this narrow strip of land that the Indians settled. Here the sea and the rivers provided an abundance of food. The dense forests—especially the cedar and the redwood—provided just about everything else.

The people of the region were expert woodworkers. They cut down the trees with elkhorn chisels and split them into planks with stone mauls and yew-wood wedges. They smoothed out the wood with an adz, a tool with a wooden handle and a bone blade.

They built large rectangular plank houses, usually with a gabled, or triangular, roof. These homes usually housed several families. People who belonged to the same clan lived together. A clan was a group of families with the same ancestor. That ancestor—an animal, a bird, or a person—was the clan's totem.

The men also built dugout canoes in many different sizes. The largest were over sixty feet long and eight feet wide! Most were made of white cedar. Because this wood splits easily, it had to be dug out a little at a time. The larger canoes took a team of two men about six months to complete. They were beautifully crafted and provided an excellent system of water transportation.

To catch the salmon, herring, cod, and halibut, many different devices were used: hooks of bone and wood, wooden spears, traps, and sometimes even clubs. The fish was baked, steamed, broiled, and boiled. It was so plentiful—especially the salmon—that much of it was dried and stored to last the winter.

Although the richness of the sea brought prosperity to the region, it also brought war. Every inch of ground and coastal waters was owned. Only families with ownership rights could hunt, fish, or gather there. Because so little land was available, fighting over the land was common. They built huge warships from which bows and arrows and even paddles were used as weapons. In close battle, warriors fought with spears, knives and daggers.

The climate was mild and rainy, and little clothing was usually worn. Basketry hats and poncho-like capes of woven cedar bark were often used as protection from the rain. For ceremonial occasions beautiful fringed robes woven by the Chilkat Indians were highly prized. These blankets were made of mountain-goat wool and cedar-bark fiber. Designs of bears, whales, and other figures were woven in. Dance skirts, woven in a similar way, had puffin beaks sewn on so that they would make sounds as the dancers moved.

Nose decorations were popular. Those who could afford it wore circles of rare shells; others made do with polished wooden rods. Some women wore labrets—plugs of shell, bone, or wood—in a slit in their lower lip. Tattooing was also common. Most women had at least a few vertical chin stripes.

The people believed that every animal and person had a soul that became a ghost after death. The shaman's job was to encourage the good spirits and to control the evil ones. To catch and heal lost souls he used a soul catcher, a tube of wood or bone open at both ends. He performed elaborate ceremonies in which he wore skillfully carved masks to represent the spirits. Some of the masks were moveable. When a string was pulled, the outer mask opened and an inner one appeared. It gave the impression that the demon had changed form.

The culture of the Northwest Coast was a rich one, based upon easy access to the sea, rivers, and forests. The sea provided more than enough food. The forests provided the materials for their homes, transportation, tools, weapons, clothing, and a rich heritage of arts and crafts.

Salmon Sacrifice

Pacific salmon breed in a river. When they spawn, or deposit their eggs, they die. The young fish, after passing through various stages of development, become parr. For two years these parr remain in the river. Then they find their way downstream to the sea. When mature, the fish—now called salmon—swim upstream and return to the place where they were spawned. They, in turn, spawn and die.

The Indians who witnessed this unusual migration cycle did not associate the parr with the salmon. They had seen the salmon die in the river; therefore, they concluded that the salmon were immortal and had been reborn in the ocean. They believed that the salmon then swam up the river to give up their lives in order to feed mankind.

A HAIKU POEM—A haiku is an unrhymed Japanese poem. There are three lines, each with a certain number of syllables. The first line has five syllables; the second has seven; the third has five. Haiku is often used to write about something in nature. Write a haiku poem in honor of the salmon from the point of view of an Indian of the Northwest Coast.

THE SALMON

_____

_____

_____

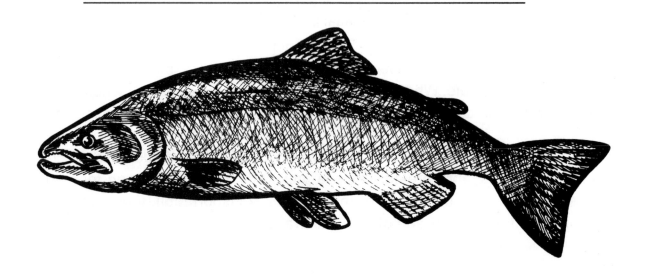

Works of Art

Northwest Coast Indians were excellent woodworkers, and the Haida were probably the best of all! They built enormous, gabled, multi-family plank houses. Many homes had carved posts surrounding them. The front post rose high above the roof and had an opening which served as a door. We call these and the other carved and painted posts totem poles. A totem pole recorded the owner's claim to fame: his ancestry, his wealth, and his ranking in the town.

The right to carve totem poles was inherited. Even the designs belonged to the family who owned the pole. If the artist made a mistake, he would be disgraced.

Figures on the totem poles and other works of art were easily recognized. A few features were used to represent the entire animal. Beaver was shown with two large front teeth and crossed lines on the tail. Wolf always had a long nose and large teeth. Raven had a long, straight beak. Bear was represented by a short snout and a protruding tongue.

The people of the Northwest Coast liked symmetry. Often the figure of the animal was split down the middle and opened out. The artists preferred not to leave any empty spaces. Sometimes they even painted in the animals bones, giving the viewer an "x-ray" view.

RAVEN   BEAR   BEAVER

A Totem Pole

A totem pole recorded a person's ancestry, wealth, and standing in the town. Decorate this totem pole to show important facts about your family. Keep in mind such things as your ancestors, prized possessions, outside interests, sports, and the various roles you play in your school or community.

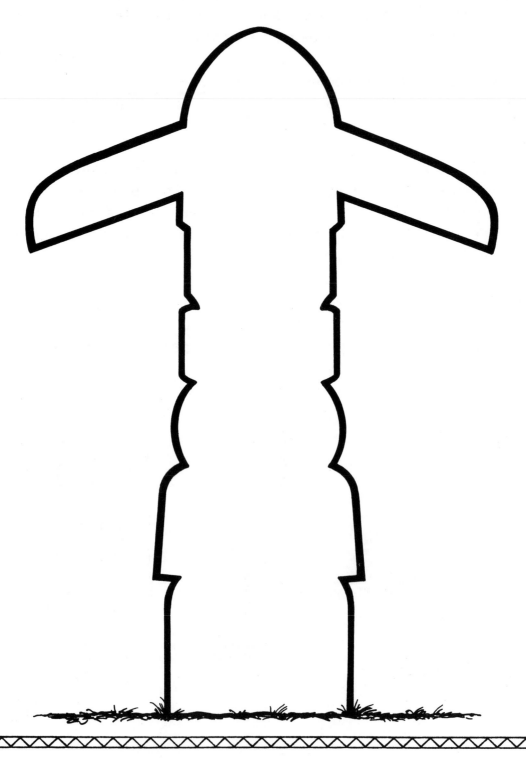

Display of Wealth

Along the Northwest Coast power was based upon wealth. There was a class system of chiefs, nobles, commoners and—lowest of all—slaves. In fact, every individual had a rank; the closer one was related to the group's legendary ancestor, or totem, the higher one's rank. Wealth included not only material possessions, but also inherited rights. These included fishing, hunting, and other territorial rights; the right to practice carving and other crafts; and the right to say certain prayers. These rights were sometimes bought and sold.

Potlatches at which the chief gave away many possessions were the most impressive displays of wealth. They were given to announce important events, such as the inheritance of a chieftainship, the marriage of a high ranking person, the completion of a house, or the raising of a totem pole. The main reason, however, was to give the chief a chance to impress everyone with his wealth.

Huge amounts of food were served in carved feast dishes, some the size of a canoe! Gifts were given out to the guests in order of their rank. The higher the rank, the more splendid the gift! Large, shield-like sheets of copper were prized as symbols of wealth. Sometimes the host gave away a "copper." Other times he broke one or two—just to show he could afford it. Slaves, too, were considered property. The chief often killed a few to show that the loss of these valuable possessions meant nothing to him.

The invited chiefs were expected to repay their host within a year. If not, they would be disgraced and so would the people of their villages. The prestige of the villagers was dependent upon that of their chief!

Potlatch Party

You are having a potlatch for 10 people. Whom will you invite?

_____   _____

_____   _____

_____   _____

_____   _____

_____   _____

On what basis will you rank them?

_____

_____

What will you give to each? Start with the highest ranked; work your way down.

_____   _____

_____   _____

_____   _____

_____   _____

_____   _____

Design your invitation here. Use a Northwest Coast motif.

What's Your Worth?

A collage is a work of art made by gluing pieces of different material to a surface. Make a collage of the items that were considered part of a person's wealth among the Indians of the Northwest Coast. You may use original artwork, pictures from magazines, and/or other materials. Use a sheet of heavy paper or board to make your collage.

A Word Search

The names of several language groups of the Northwest Coast and other terms relating to the Northwest Coast culture area are hidden in this word search. Look up and down, backwards and forwards, and diagonally in all directions to find them.

LANGUAGE GROUPS:
(From north to south along the coast):

- Tlingit
- Haida
- Tsimshian
- Bella Coola
- Kwakiutl
- Nootka
- Coast Salish
- Quileute
- Chinook

OTHER TERMS:

- Copper
- Potlatch
- Raven
- Salmon
- Totem

```
B B A C O D C O M P U T C I N E V A R D A T S
E X A Y U H A I D A O G R M T G O L A N A O T
L P J U T H L K F M A R G O R P I M E L E S O
L G O S D L O S D A E H N M A K R I C M A T P
A R A T D N I H I R E L T U I K A W K L N I R
C E T F L F C N F H O R D L A R E C M I D K I
O M E T O A H M G X E N R O F E U O R S I O O
O M P W B Z T X H I O E N R T K N P E O N O N
L A R A B P R C E G T R C U S T P U T F P N L
A R R R O R T A H U P M E N O O T K A T U I I
P G O O C O A S T S A L I S H C P E I W R H N
A O C T T A A M I C I P A I T I E R A A O C E
T R E N C S O C I U C U B C O P P E R R F G L
A P O O N C E T Q B O T S I M S H I A N L S M
D L A T O T E M E D F B L R A B T M T D O A R
```

The Nootka Whalers

Once in a while a village would be lucky enough to find a dead whale along the shore. It provided a great source of oil, meat, bone, and sinew. Among the few to actually hunt the whale, however, were the Nootka. They went out in small fleets of about four or five canoes. It was very dangerous.

The chief was the first to thrust his harpoon into the whale. The crew members followed. Sealskin drags were attached to the line to tire out the whale. Sometimes the whale pulled forty or fifty drags before it was exhausted enough to be speared.

Endangered Animals

Many species of whales are now considered endangered. That means they are in danger of becoming extinct—of no longer existing!

List at least ten other animals that are considered to be endangered.

_____   _____
_____   _____
_____   _____
_____   _____
_____   _____

Design a poster that would encourage people to help an endangered species.

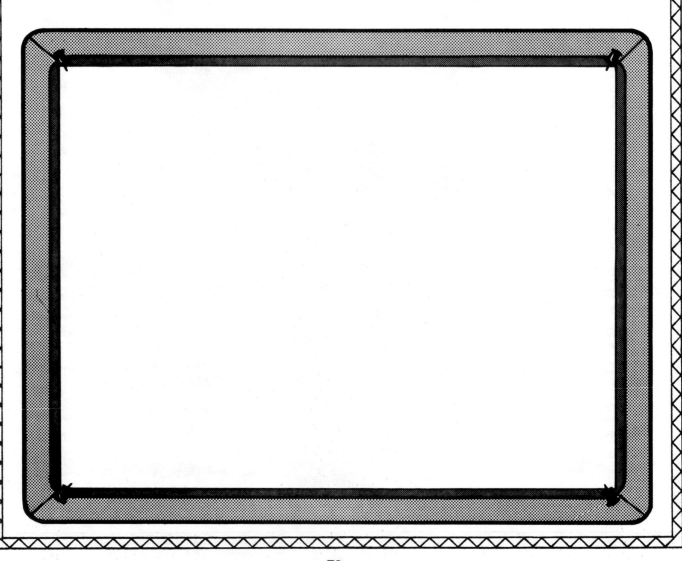

The People of the Sub-Arctic

The Sub-Arctic covered a large area, but it was not highly populated. The eastern tribes, such as the Cree and the Ojibwa, spoke Algonquian dialects. The western tribes, such as the Slave, the Yellowknife, the Beaver, the Carrier, and the Kutchin spoke Athabascan.

It was a land of brief summers and long, cold winters. In fact, winters sometimes lasted over eight months! Temperatures occasionally got as low as −80°F (−62°C). It was not surprising that relatively few people lived in this harsh environment. Those who did depended upon hunting, fishing, and gathering. Moose, beaver, and—above all—caribou were the most important game.

Except for the short summer, the Indians of the Sub-Arctic had to face their greatest foe—the weather. In order to survive, they learned to adapt to that severe environment. Unlike tribes in the other regions, the people of the Sub-Arctic often wore tailored clothing. Trousers and moccasins were sometimes made in a single piece. Extra layers of caribou skins were added to their homes during the winter for extra warmth. In the northernmost part of Alaska, they built their winter homes partly underground. The deep snow served as an insulator against the bitter cold. Throughout the Sub-Arctic toboggans or sleds and snowshoes were absolute necessities! It wasn't easy, but the people did the best they could with what they had.

Syllogisms

In a valid argument the conclusion must be **in agreement with** and **based upon** the previous statements. Decide whether the following arguments are valid (V) or invalid (I).

1. A. All major tribes of the eastern Sub-Arctic spoke Algonquian dialects.
   B. The Cree were an important tribe of the eastern Sub-Arctic.
   C. Therefore, the Cree spoke Algonquian.

   Valid or Invalid: _____

2. A. All major tribes of the western Sub-Arctic spoke Athabascan.
   B. The Chipewyan spoke Athabascan.
   C. Therefore, the Chipewyan lived in the western Sub-Arctic.

   Valid or Invalid: _____

3. A. Many hunting tribes were nomadic.
   B. The Chipewyans were a hunting tribe.
   C. Therefore, the Chipewyans were nomadic.

   Valid or Invalid: _____

4. A. Snowshoes were used by all Sub-Arctic tribes.
   B. The Kutchin were a Sub-Arctic tribe.
   C. Therefore, the Kutchins used snowshoes.

   Valid or Invalid: _____

5. A. The Chipewyans, who lived in the Sub-Arctic, used tepees covered with caribou skins.
   B. The Shuswap lived in the Sub-Arctic.
   C. Therefore, the Shuswap used tepees covered with caribou skins.

   Valid or Invalid: _____

Now make up two syllogisms of your own about Native Americans. Exchange them with your classmates to solve.

Fun and Games

Like most peoples, Native Americans enjoyed playing games. A few popular games were the hoop-and-pole game, snowsnake, and many kinds of guessing games. People often bet on the results.

A version of the hoop-and-pole game was played by males in just about every tribe. Usually, two players ran down the course. As they ran, one rolled a hoop ahead of them. When the hoop reached a certain point, the players slid their poles along the ground. The object was to land the pole in a way that the hoop would fall across it when it stopped rolling. Points were determined by how the poles landed in relation to the hoop.

Snowsnake was played after a deep accumulation of snow. If near a frozen lake or river, a path was cleared over the thick ice. If not, they stomped down on the snow or dragged a log along it until a smooth, compact trail—about 1,500 feet long—was made. Each player took a turn hurling his tapered stick as far along the path as he could. The stick, which was carefully smoothed, was called a snowsnake because it resembled a snake as it traveled. Sometimes its front end was carved to look like a snake's head.

Both men and women loved guessing games. The moccasin game, played with two teams of three, was popular with the men. A small object was placed under each of four moccasins; one object was marked. A player from the opposing team guessed which moccasin covered the marked object. The teams alternated placing the objects and doing the guessing. They kept track of the score with wooden tallies.

The women enjoyed the counting game. One version called for two teams of two. A woman from one team tossed a tray with pitch-filled shells. A woman from the other team guessed how may shells would land pitch side up when caught on the tray. The teams alternated tossing and guessing. A fifth woman usually tallied the score with sticks.

A New Game

Invent a game in which all of the equipment is made from natural materials.

What is the object of your game?

_____

_____

How many players can participate? Is it a team game?

_____

_____

Is the game co-ed? Is there an age requirement? If so, why?

_____

_____

Give your game a name. List at least five rules of your game.

Rules of _____.

1.

2.

3.

4.

5.

On another sheet of paper draw a picture of your game being played.

More
Critical & Creative
Thinking-Skill
Activities

Scrambled Foods

Corn, beans, squash and many of the other foods we eat originated with the Indians of North, Central and South America. Unscramble the letters and find out the names of some of those foods!

1. **V A C O O A D**   _____

2. **N U S F L W O R E   E E D S S**   _____

3. **A M I Z E**   _____

4. **U S A S Q H**   _____

5. **D I W L   R R E H C I E S**   _____

6. **W E E T S   A T S O T E P O**   _____

7. **S E O T A M O T**   _____

8. **E P A L M   A G U S R**   _____

9. **A P E U N T**   _____

10. **T C O C O H L A E**   _____

11. **M U P K N I P**   _____

76

Mobile Magic

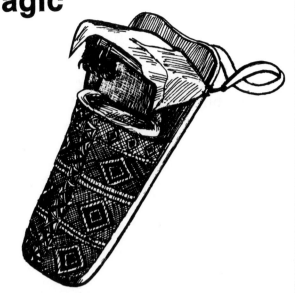

In some tribes bear claws or small bows and arrows were hung from the cradleboard of an infant boy. The boy's parents hoped it would help the child grow up with the desire to be a brave hunter and warrior.

Pretend that you are a parent. Design a mobile to be hung above the crib of your infant boy or girl. The mobile should instill in the child traits that you consider desirable.

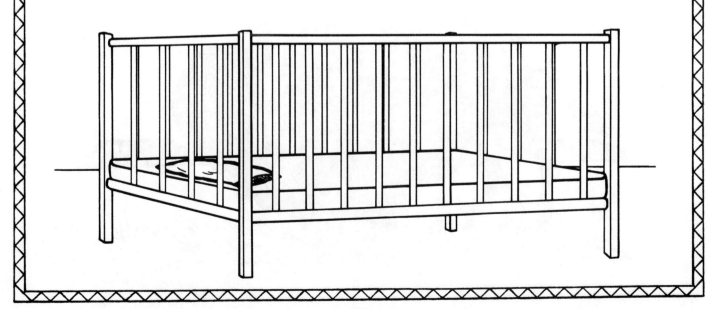

Waste Not, Want Not

The Buffalo was the "life blood" of the Plains Indians. Just about every bit was used. Stretch your imagination. List all the ways in which the various parts of the buffalo were utilized.

Home, Sweet Home

The tribes of North America had many different lifestyles. Some were farmers; some were fishers; some were hunters; and some were gatherers. The areas they inhabited had different soil, different climates, and different food supplies. It was only natural that the homes they lived in would differ too.

In the Northeast Woodlands the Algonquian hunters lived in wigwams, while the Iroquois farmers lived in longhouses. The Seminoles of Florida built open stilt houses, called chickees. The Mandan farmers of the northern Plains had large earth lodges. The buffalo hunters of the Plains lived in portable tepees. People in the Basin-Plateau region lived in huts called wickiups. The Haida of the Northwest Coast lived in finely crafted plank houses. Each tribe used what the land provided to make homes that best suited its way of life.

Think about your home. How does it fit your family's lifestyle? Is there anything you would change to better suit the needs of your family?

_____

_____

_____

_____

_____

Draw a picture showing a change you would like to make in your house.

To Each His Own

Research a North American Indian tribe of your choice. Write a brief report that explains how the customs, homes, clothing, arts and crafts, etc., fit the people's lifestyle and environment. Draw a picture or make a diorama to go with your report.

Eulogy to a Great Man: Tecumseh

The Shawnee leader Tecumseh was a great statesman, warrior and orator. Considered by many to be the greatest and wisest of all Indian leaders, Tecumseh dreamed of a separate Indian nation in which all tribes would unite as one People. His vision raised the hopes of many, but—although it came close—it never came to be.

Tecumseh preached that Indian land belonged to all the tribes in common. He once said, "No tribe has the right to sell, even to each other, much less to strangers, who demand all, and will take no less.... Sell a country! Why not sell the air, the clouds, and the great sea as well as the earth? Did not the Great Spirit make them all for the use of his children?"*

Tecumseh joined forces with the British during the War of 1812. On October 5, 1813, he died in battle against United States troops, which were led by William Henry Harrison. With him died his cause and his dream of a united Indian Confederation.

Research Tecumseh. Compose a eulogy (a speech in praise of someone) to be read at a memorial service for him.

*See Josephy, Alvin M. (New York: Viking Press, 1961), p. 155.

We're All Human

Create a poster to encourage people not to stereotype any ethnic group. Sketch your ideas on a separate sheet of paper.

Now evaluate the ideas you sketched. Which one will you choose for your poster? Follow these instructions to help you decide:

1. Write a short description of each idea.
   List the descriptions in the "Poster Ideas" column.
2. Identify 5 criteria by which to judge the ideas.
   Write them in the spaces provided.
3. Judge how each idea meets the criteria you have set.
   Use the scale to rate each idea.
4. Total the points.
   Figure out which idea best meets your criteria.
5. Decide which idea you will use for your poster.

SCALE:

5 = Excellent
4 = Good
3 = Okay
2 = Fair
1 = Poor

CRITERIA

TOTAL

POSTER IDEAS

Best idea: _____

Reasons why: _____

_____

_____

_____

_____

_____

_____

Now create a poster using the idea you chose!

Native Americans
Crossword Puzzle

Across

4. Tried to create a united Indian Nation.
5. Important to Plains Indians.
9. Cherokee's trek, the Trail of _____.
11. Wedges, axes and chisels.
12. Home of the Sioux and the Cheyenne.
13. Made from quahog shells.
14. Warrior's was decorated with brave deeds.
15. Climate along Northwest Coast.
16. Represented by feather on war bonnet.
20. Provided abundance of food along NW Coast.
22. Invented Cherokee alphabet.
26. Important material of Northeast Woodlands.
28. Used to make spoons.
29. Iroquois women.
32. Maize.
34. Used for hunting.
35. First person singular of verb "to be."
37. Region where Creeks lived (abbrev.).
38. Part of buffalo used to make tools.
39. Built plank houses.
41. Salmon, for example.
43. Scarce in Southwest.
44. Northwest tribe that wore armor in battle.
45. Important in Northwestern folklore.
49. A harsh environment.
50. Major form of water transportation.
52. Their name means "The Peaceful Ones."
53. Its teeth were used to decorate dresses.
56. Where Haida lived is now this country.
57. People of the Longhouse.
59. Useful tree in Northwest.
60. _____ nations in League (with Tuscarora).

Down

1. Dyed ones used for decoration.
2. Chief Joseph's tribe.
3. Feast at which gifts were given out.
4. Carved post of Northwest Coast.
6. Important food source of Northwest Coast.
7. Used with 34 across.
8. Lived in hogans.
10. Collected in troughs.
16. Creek tribes formed this.
17. You and me.
18. Buffalo meat and berry mixture.
19. Used to pull travois before horses.
21. Skin footware.
23. Used to build pueblos.
24. Interjection used to express emotion.
25. In Southeast often made of cane.
26. California women were especially good at it.
27. Hogan, wigwam and tepee.
30. A surprise attack.
31. Tool used to punch holes.
33. Home to Senecas and Mohegans (abbrev.).
36. Pueblos painted theirs with earth colors.
39. Legendary founder of Iroquois League.
40. Language of the Chipewyans.
42. Its introduction changed life on the Plains.
46. Algonquian home.
47. Coup sticks used in this.
48. Where 10 down comes from.
51. Pueblo man or Navajo woman.
54. Religious place of Pueblos.
55. Pueblo-dwelling tribe.
58. Natchez ruler, the Great _____.

Native American Patriots

Design a block of commemorative stamps to honor four Native American patriots (from the Native American point of view!).

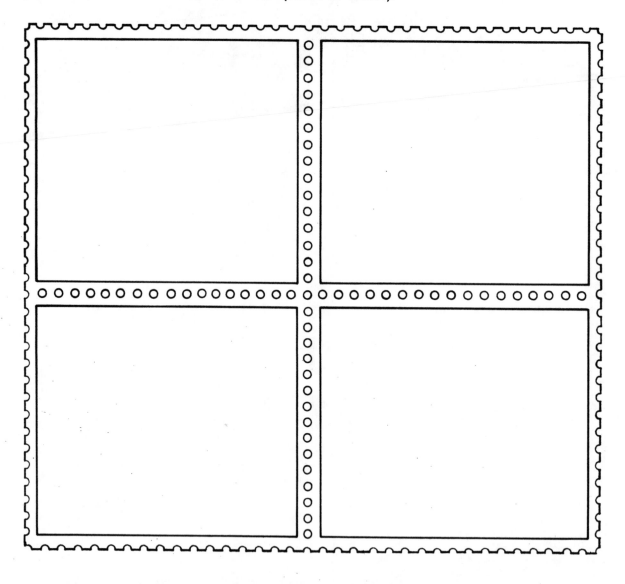

Write a paragraph explaining why you chose those four.

_____

_____

_____

_____

_____

ANSWERS

Many of the activities call for original, creative answers; answers to those activities will vary greatly and are not given here.

Page 7: Beyond a Reasonable Doubt
The log is 5,700 years old. The following are among the problems that might arise: It is not always clear—as it was in the case of the Folsom point found between the ribs of the Ice Age bison—that the artifact was in clear association with the plant or animal remains used to test it. Digging animals, landslides, etc. can mix up the stratigraphy (layers) of a site. Also, what appears to be the work of humans might be the result of nature or the work of another animal.

Page 16: Hidden Foods
1. deer   2. maple   3. corn   4. clam   5. caribou
6. bear   7. beans   8. nut   9. fish   10. rabbit

Page 19: A Symbol of the League
There are many symbols. A few examples are the arrows used to indicate recyling; the peace symbol; the skull and crossbones representing danger or poison; the polar bear as a symbol of endangered species; and a white flag as a sign of surrender.

Page 40: What Did You Say?
The many tribes of the Plains spoke dialects of six distinct language families. Even within the same language family, it was often difficult to understand members of another tribe. The Plains Indians developed a system to help them communicate with one another. By using a fixed set of hand and finger positions, they could get across their ideas. Sign language was especially important in intertribal activities. Those of the same tribe might have used sign language if they did not want to be overheard or if they were too far apart to hear each other.

Page 47: The Snake Ceremony
Most of the ceremonies of the Southwest had the same object: to entice the gods to bring rain. For this ceremony snakes were collected from the four cardinal points, the Four Winds . For nine days they were washed, prayed over, and purified in the kiva. They were then brought out to participate in the dance. After the dance the snakes were brought back to the desert and released. It was hoped that they would act as messengers to the Four Winds, whom they would beg for rain.

Page 51: Find Those Words
The 90 + words include the following: a, ace, ale, alms, are, arm, as, calm, came, car, care, case, cease, clam, clear, close, come, core, cram, cream, crease, coarse, eagle, ear, earl, ease, easel, eel, elm, else, em, en, era, erase, lace, lame, lease, lee, leer, loam, lore, lose, mace, male, mar, mare, me, meal, mere, molar, mole, moral, morale, more, oar, or, oracle, ore, race, ram, real, realm, ream, reel, roam, roe, role, rose, sale, same, scale, scam, scar, scare, score, scram, sea, seal, seam, sear, see, seem, seer, slam, smear, soar, sole, some, and sore.

Page 53: Coyote Makes Man
The code is as follows: A-Z, B-Y, C-X, D-W, E-V, F-U, G-T, H-S, I-R, J-Q, K-P, L-O, M-N, N-M, O-L, P-K, Q-J, R-I, S-H, T-G, U-F, V-E, W-D, X-C, Y-B, and Z-A. This is how the legend reads: Coyote wished to create man. He called all the animals of earth together to ask their advice. Each told the features it thought should be given. Lion suggested a voice that can roar, sharp teeth and claws. Grizzly Bear suggested great strength. Deer suggested beautiful long horns, while Mountain Goat suggested that the horns be rolled. Owl suggested wings, and Mouse suggested sharp eyes. Coyote listened to the advice. "All of you are very foolish," he said. "You all want to make man like yourselves. Man should be these things," he agreed, "but he should also be as wise as I am." The animals each worked to make man out of clay. Each tried to make man look like himself. But before they could finish, they all fell asleep. Coyote threw water on the clay figures and they all melted away. By the time the animals awakened, Coyote had created man. He had given to man the best part of each of the animals.

Page 67: What's Your Worth?
A person's wealth included material belongings such as canoes, clothing, blankets, bowls, homes, coppers, tools and weapons, etc. It also included fishing and hunting rights, the right to practice carving and other crafts, the right to say certain prayers, and the right to sing certain songs. It also included the person's slaves.

Page 68: A Word Search

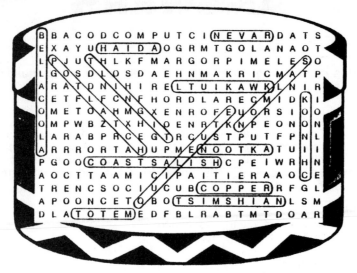

Page 70: Endangered Animals
A few endangered animals are the African elephant, the green turtle, the grizzly bear, the cheetah, the mountain gorilla, and the Siberian tiger. For a current list, contact the Office of Endangered Species, U.S. Department of the Interior, Fish and Wildlife Service, Washington, D.C. 20240.

Page 72: Syllogisms
1. V   2. I   3. I   4. V   5. I

Page 76: Scrambled Foods
1. avocado   2. sunflower seeds   3. maize   4. squash   5. wild cherries
6. sweet potatoes   7. tomatoes   8. maple sugar   9. chocolate   10. pumpkin

Page 78: Waste Not, Want Not
The following are some of the ways in which the buffalo was used: the meat—food, including pemmican; hides—tepees, clothing (shirts, dresses, leggings, robes), moccasins, blankets, shields, winter counts, parfleches, and medicine bundles; sinew—bowstrings and laces; shoulder bones—hoes; rib bones—runners for dog sleds and children's sleds; porous bones—paint brushes; horns—cups, spoons, and bowls; and dried dung (buffalo chips)—fuel.

Page 85: A Crossword Puzzle

```
              Q      N                    P
        TECUMSEH   BUFFALO                O
    N       O     I        Z       I      R      T
TEARS   TOOLS   PLAINS        R      L
    V       A     L        E        H      O      A
WAMPUM        SHIRT              W E      T
    J             C                S      C
COUP      D      SEA       M              H
O  SEQUOYA                 O        O      K
N   M      D        BIRCH   HORN
FARMERS   O    A        CORN       I
    E    I   A     BOWS   S    A M    E   P   F
    D    C   I     ELK    K    SE    BONE
    E  HAIDA          E   FISH        T
RAIN    TLINGIT      N    O        T
    A       A      H       R  S    RAVEN
    C       W      A       W  Y    W    S    R
    Y   A   M  BASIN    CANOE        Y
        T   A      A       G  W    R
        HOPIS      W  ELK          Z
        A   L   CANADA    IROQUOIS
            E      A   M    V  V        N    U
            N            CEDAR  SIX     N
            R
```

Page 86: Native American Patriots
Some suggestions are Hiawatha, King Philip, Pope, Pontiac, Seattle, Tecumseh, Osceola, Chief Joseph, Black Hawk, Red Cloud, Joseph Brandt, Sequoya, John Ross, and Sitting Bull.